IS IT REAL?

Pauline Cartwright
Toby Quarmby

Some things are real.

We can see them.
We can touch them.

Some things
are not real.

We cannot see them.
We cannot touch them.

Is this horse real?

Yes!

We can see it.
We can touch it.

Is this real?

No!

It is not real.

This is a horse.

This is a unicorn.

It would be fun
if unicorns were real!

Is this fish real?

Yes!

We can see it.
We can touch it.

Is this real?

It is not real.

This is a fish.

This is a mermaid.

It would be fun
if mermaids were real!

Is this lizard real?

Yes!

We can see it.
We can touch it.

Is this real?

No!

It is not real.

This is a lizard.

This is a dragon.

Would it be fun
if dragons were real?

It would **not** be fun
if dragons were real!